The Laird of Cockpen

The Laird of Cockpen

by SORCHE NIC LEODHAS

illustrated by ADRIENNE ADAMS

Holt, Rinehart and Winston   NEW YORK   CHICAGO   SAN FRANCISCO

Books for Young People by Sorche Nic Leodhas

The Laird of Cockpen   Ghosts Go Haunting
Kellyburn Braes   Gaelic Ghosts
Sea-Spell and Moor-Magic   All in the Morning Early
Claymore and Kilt   Thistle and Thyme
Always Room for One More   Heather and Broom

Text Copyright © 1969 by Leclaire G. Alger.
Illustrations Copyright © 1969 by Adrienne Adams.
All rights reserved, including the right to reproduce this book
or portions thereof in any form.
Published simultaneously in Canada by Holt, Rinehart and Winston
of Canada, Limited.
SBN: 03-071750-7
Library of Congress Catalog Card Number: 68-19993
Printed in the United States of America
First Edition

Another for the Toiseach
Allan Digby

The Laird of Cockpen, he's proud and he's great;
His mind's taken up with the things of the state;
He wanted a wife his braw house to keep,
But favor with wooing was fashious to seek.

Down by the dyke-side a lady did dwell,
At his table-head he thought she'd look well;
M'Clish's sole daughter of Claversehall Lea—
A penniless lass with a long pedigree.

His wig was well-powdered as good as when new,
His waistcoat was white, his coat it was blue.
He put on a ring, a sword, and cocked hat—
And who could refuse the Laird with all that?

He took the gray mare and rode cannily,
And rapped at the gate of Claversehall Lea;
"Go tell Mistress Jean to come speedily in,
She's wanted to speak to the Laird of Cockpen."

Mistress Jean she was making the elder-flower wine;
"And what brings the Laird at such a like time?"

She put off her apron and on her silk gown,
Her mutch with red ribbons, and went away down.

And when she came in, she bowed full low;
And what was his errand he soon let her know.
Amazed was the Laird when the lady said "Nay!"
And with a low curtsy she then turned away.

Dumbfoundered he was, but no sign did she see;
He mounted his mare and rode off cannily;
And often he thought as he rode through the glen,
"She's daft to refuse the Laird of Cockpen."

And now that the Laird his exit had made,
Mistress Jean reflected on what she had said;
"Oh, for one I'll get better, it's worse I'd get ten—
I was daft to refuse the Laird of Cockpen!"

Next time that the Laird and the Lady were seen,
They were going arm and arm to the kirk on the green;

Now she sits in his hall like a weel-tappit hen,
For now she is wed to the Laird of Cockpen.

About the Song

LADY NAIRNE was born in Perthshire, Scotland, on the sixteenth of July, 1766. Her father, Lord Nairne, was one of the devoted followers of the Stuarts in their attempt to recover the crown of Scotland. He took part in the uprising of 1745-46, and after the defeat at Culloden was in the party of Bonnie Prince Charley, and escaped with him to France where he remained in exile for seventeen years. Lord Nairne was pardoned and his estates restored in 1764. Two years after his return to Scotland his daughter, Lady Nairne, was born and he named her Caroline in honor of the prince he loved so well.

Lady Nairne received an excellent education and grew up to be a beautiful, sweet, and gentle woman, and so kind to the poor and unfortunate that she was known far and wide as the "Flower of Strathearn." She began writing songs at a very early age, but as she wrote under a penname it was years before the identity of the author of the songs, which were immensely popular, was known. The discovery was made when her publishers brought out a collected volume of the melodies and gave her name as author of the words. Many of her songs are still sung, and among them are "The Auld House," "The Land o' the Leal," "The Hundred Pipers an A', an A'," "There Grows a Bonny Brier Bush," and the version of "Hunting-Tower" which is best-known today.

The Laird of Cockpen is founded upon an incident that came to Lady Nairne's notice about the wooing and rejection of a laird in her own neighborhood. In her version, Lady Nairne left the laird dumbfoundered and rejected, but the novelist, Mrs. Ferrier, wanted a happy ending so she added the two last stanzas to Lady Nairne's song, and got the Laird and the Lady wedded at last. All of Lady Nairne's songs were written in the Doric, or "braid Scots" dialect, so it was thought best to change many of the Scottish words in *The Laird of Cockpen* into English so that they would be more easily understood.

The tune to which this song was written is one of the oldest Scottish melodies in existence. The name of the composer has been long lost, but the name of the air itself has survived through all the years. It is called, "When She Cam' Ben She Bobbit Fu' Laigh" and Lady Nairne has made use of these words in one of the stanzas of her own song.

1. The Laird of Cock-pen, he's proud and he's great; His
2. Down by the dyke-side a la - dy did dwell, At his

mind's tak-en up with the things of the state; He
ta - ble - head he thought she'd look well; M'-

want-ed a wife his braw house to keep, But
Clish'-s sole daugh-ter of Cla-verse-hall Lea — A

fa - vor with woo - ing was fash-ious to seek.
pen - ni - less lass with a long ped - i - gree.

A Note about the Song: We have given the tune with the first two verses; the singer should adapt the tune in a similar way to the rest of the verses.

Glossary

Braw: Brave. A braw thing is splendid, showy, or grand.

Cannily: Jauntily. Smartly.

Daft: Crazy. Foolish. Silly.

Dyke-side: A dyke is a raised road or causeway built above marshy ground; to dwell by the dyke-side, would be to live by such a road.

Fashious: Troublesome. Vexatious.

Kirk: Church.

Laird: A Laird is a lord, the owner of a landed estate or a manor, and his title is granted by the Crown.

Mutch: A mutch is a bonnet, usually white, with a high crown, a band, usually decorated with bright ribbons if the wearer was young, and with black ribbons, if worn by an older woman. A mutch often had a fluted frill attached to the band close about the face.

Weel-tappit hen: A weel-tappit hen is one that is plump and well-cared for. Tappit actually means "cockaded" and implies a jaunty pride, in one's life and surroundings.

ABOUT THE ARTIST: One of the most distinguished and respected names in the field of children's book illustration, Adrienne Adams has twice been runner-up for the Caldecott Medal, with *The Day We Saw the Sun Come Up* and *Houses from the Sea* by Alice E. Goudey. *Cabbage Moon* by Jan Wahl, *The Twelve Dancing Princesses* by Andrew Lang, and *The White Rat's Tale* by Barbara Schiller, are other fine examples of the exquisite line, beautiful color, and imaginative, fairytale quality for which her work is known. Miss Adams was born in Arkansas and educated at Stephens College and the University of Missouri. She and her husband, author John Lonzo Anderson, live on twenty-seven acres of woodland in New Jersey.

ABOUT THE BOOK: The book is set in Weiss Roman and was printed by offset. Adrienne Adams' illustrations are watercolor paintings.